Everything You Need To Know About

TEEN SUICIDE

Every year, teen suicide brings tragedy to the lives of thousands of friends and families of suicide victims.

· THE NEED TO KNOW LIBRARY ·

Everything You Need To Know About

TEEN SUICIDE

Jay Schleifer

THE ROSEN PUBLISHING GROUP, INC.
NEW YORK

Published in 1988, 1991, 1993, 1997, 1999 by The Rosen Publishing Group, Inc.
29 East 21st Street, New York, NY 10010

Revised Edition 1999

Library of Congress Cataloging-in-Publication Data

Schleifer, Jay
    Everything you need to know about teen suicide / Jay Schleifer.
      p. cm.—(The need to know library)
    Includes bibliographical references and index.
    Summary: Examines reasons why young people kill themselves, how to recognize when friends are in such trouble, and how to help potential suicide victims.
    ISBN 0-8239-3038-6
    1. Teenagers—United States—Suicidal behavior—Juvenile literature.
2. Suicide—United States—Prevention—Juvenile literature. [1. Suicide] I. Title.
II. Series.
HV6546.S36 1988
362.2—dc19   88-6636
                                                             CIP
                                                              AC

Manufactured in the United States of America

Contents

Introduction

When clicking sounds woke Jordon at 3:30 in the morning, he couldn't figure out what was going on. As the haze of sleep cleared, he realized what he was hearing. His older sister, Kerry, was on her computer in the middle of the night again. It was just the latest weird behavior by sixteen-year-old Kerry.

The changes had begun when their parents had split up and Mom had moved them to California from their small town back East. At first Jordon had hated moving. But in time he had made new friends and had even started to like his new school.

Not Kerry. She seemed to lose all interest in life. She made no new friends and mostly moped around the house. Jordon knew that she was skipping school and getting drunk on liquor from the downstairs cabinet. He wouldn't tell Mom, of course; he wasn't a snitch. But he did tell Kerry that she was messing up her life. "You're not giving it a chance," he said. "It's not so bad here."

All he got from Kerry was a cold stare and a short answer: "I'd rather be dead than live here."

Then one morning, Kerry seemed to be in a better mood. It seemed like she had settled something in her mind.

She handed Jordon a slip of paper. "I know you've always wanted my computer, Jordy. Well, good news. It's yours. Here's the password." Then, with an odd smile, she turned and walked upstairs.

That night her family would find the long, desperate e-mails from Kerry to her friends back East, telling them how miserable she was in this new place. They would also discover that Kerry had visited Web site after Web site about death and dying. But it was too late. That day, Kerry had stolen sleeping pills from her mother's medicine cabinet and had swallowed them all in one fatal dose.

Today suicide is the third leading cause of death for young people between the ages of fifteen and twenty-four. Suicide is the second leading cause of death among high school and college students. And the number of young people who kill themselves is not getting any smaller.

This book explores some reasons behind the growing number of teen suicides. It also explains how to help prevent yourself and others from becoming one of these tragic statistics.

Like Jordon, people often don't know how serious a problem is until it is too late. Many teen suicides could be prevented if people were more aware of the reasons for suicide, its warning signs, and the best ways to approach someone who may be suicidal. Teens who don't know how to cope with the difficulties in their lives may consider suicide as a way to end their problems. What they don't realize is that there are other ways to address what is causing them pain. This book suggests alternative methods of dealing with problems and lists many of the resources available to help teens learn how to cope.

There are many common ideas about suicide that are not true. These myths can be very dangerous. Knowing the right thing to do when someone is in danger of committing suicide may mean being able to avoid these mistakes. Chapter one discusses some of these popular myths.

People often have trouble understanding why so many teens would want to kill themselves. Chapter two explains how both teens and adults can have an extremely difficult time coping with emotions and could begin to think of suicide as a solution.

When people are considering suicide, they often give clues that they are preparing to kill themselves. This book discusses possible warning signs and how to recognize them. If you suspect that a friend or family member may be thinking about committing suicide, watch for the signs listed in chapter three.

Suicide *can* be prevented. If you are feeling depressed or overwhelmed, there are trained counselors who know the right way to talk people through their problems. Chapter four outlines the steps counselors take when talking to someone about painful emotions. It explains what counseling is for and what it is like.

It is extremely important to contact a professional if someone you know is at risk of committing suicide, but there are things that you can do as well. You should talk about the problem with a school counselor, a teacher, a suicide hotline operator, the police, or any trusted adult who is willing to listen. You may save a friend or family member's life. Chapter five will explain the things that you should—and should not—do when someone you know needs help.

If someone you know has already committed suicide, you probably have a great deal of grief and confusion to work through. This book discusses the mixed emotions that a suicide can create and suggests some methods that family and friends can use to deal with their feelings after a suicide.

With more information, teens who feel the way that Kerry did will realize that suicide is never the answer. And if they can be convinced that there is hope for the future, teens may not take the final and fatal step that Kerry did.

It can be difficult to know what to do when someone you know is feeling depressed.

Chapter 1

The Tragic Choice: Teen Suicide

Why Is Teen Suicide on the Rise?

Today only accidents and homicide claim the lives of more young people than suicide. In 1998 almost 5,000 people between the ages of fifteen and twenty-four were reported to have killed themselves.

Teens today are confronting suicide much more often than their parents did when they were young. There were three times as many teen suicides in 1998 as there were in 1950. And the rate of attempted suicide for younger teens is growing quickly. In 1998 more than twice as many young people age ten to fourteen attempted suicide as in 1988.

It's not surprising that suicide rates have increased dramatically in the last fifty years. The teen years are typically marked by feelings of insecurity and depression. Teens also have to deal with pressures from parents, peers, and society in general. Recently

11

these pressures have become even more extreme.
Illegal drug use is a much more common problem for
teens today than for past generations. A 1998 study
found that more than half of all high school students
use illegal drugs by the time they graduate. And
there is no doubt that suicide and drug use are linked:
According to another 1998 report, more than half of
all teenage suicide victims had substance abuse
problems.

In addition to the usual issues teens have faced in
the past, more and more young people are troubled by
problems that were once considered only adult con-
cerns. Complicated issues of birth control, pregnancy,
and sexually transmitted diseases (STDs) can create
further problems for teens. In addition, teens who
think they may be bisexual or gay often experience
feelings of extreme isolation and depression. As a
result, many come to consider suicide the only solution.

Many teens today are growing up in environments
where violence and crime are common. Others may
be living with abusive parents and feel unsafe in
their own homes. It may be difficult for these teens to
find a place where they can be safe or to find people
whom they can trust.

A Cry for Help

At one time, committing suicide was considered
to be a disgraceful act. In parts of Europe, there
was a time when people who killed themselves

were buried at crossroads. This was intended to draw attention and shame to the suicide. Many religions also condemn suicide. Judaism, Christianity, and Islam consider it morally wrong.

For many years, suicide was considered a crime in the United States. As the reasons why people commit suicide have become better understood, anti-suicide laws in many states have been removed. Today, suicide is outlawed in only two states. People have found that punishing someone who has attempted suicide only adds to his or her depression, which could lead to another suicide attempt.

Over time there have been more efforts to help people understand why someone would commit suicide. But sometimes when people hear about suicide they may think about copying suicide victims. There have been stories about suicides, both fictional and real, that may make suicide seem romantic or glamorous. For example, in 1594 William Shakespeare wrote the play *Romeo and Juliet,* in which the two title characters, when faced with the idea that they could not be together, committed suicide.

A more recent example is the suicide of Kurt Cobain, the lead singer of the rock band, Nirvana. Cobain had many fans. When he killed himself, some young people thought that suicide might be cool. But Cobain's wife, Courtney Love, has publicly told his fans that what her husband did was selfish and wrong. Cobain also left behind a baby who will never know her father.

Suicide is not romantic or cool. No matter how troubled a suicide victim may have been, his or her death never helps anyone. In most cases, a suicide attempt is really a cry for help. People who commit suicide often believe that their problems are too big and scary for them to ever solve. But no matter how big a problem may be, there is a better solution. And help is always available.

What Makes Teens Feel So Bad?

It is not possible to list all the reasons why teens decide to take their own lives. But here are some of the more common causes:

- Feeling rejected, abandoned, or alone
- Low self-esteem, or feeling like a failure
- Feeling ashamed and unworthy of forgiveness
- Pressures at school, home, or with friends
- Problems with alcohol or drugs
- Feelings of hopelessness or depression (sadness that does not go away and has no clear cause)
- Feeling afraid of something or someone

Often, teens who kill themselves have had upsetting experiences of some kind. Young suicide victims may explain their feelings in notes they leave behind. Some of their reasons may include:

- Breaking up with a boyfriend or girlfriend

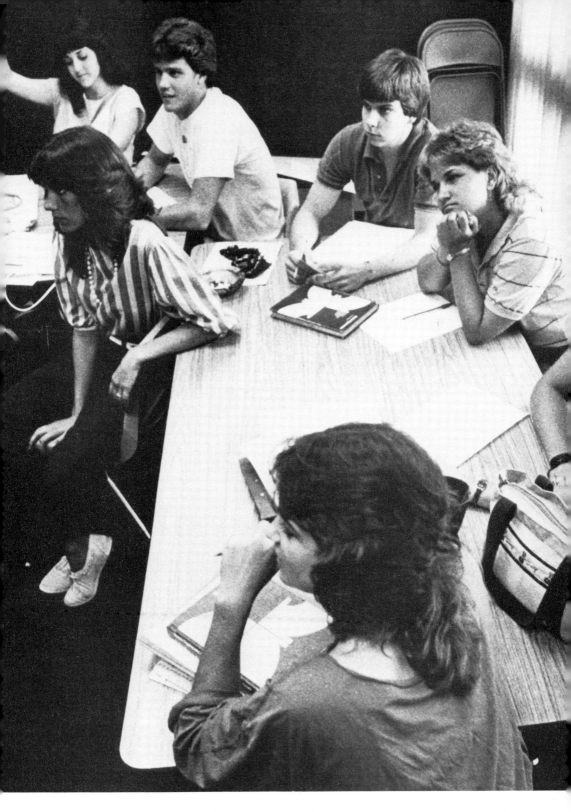

In some schools students get together to discuss common problems. It helps them to talk about the pressures or fears they may be feeling.

- Doing poorly in school, or not being accepted for a job or by a college
- Not doing well in sports or other activities
- Being gay and feeling guilty or afraid of not being accepted
- Moving and leaving friends behind, or having a good friend move away
- Divorce or other problems in the family (such as alcohol, drugs, or sexual abuse)
- Being unable to repay a large debt
- A serious physical injury or illness
- Being responsible for an injury to another person
- Having committed a serious crime
- The death of a parent, close friend, or other family member

Some of the problems that teen suicide victims list may seem much more serious than others. But all of these problems are very real to the people who experience them.

These problems can also trigger some of the uncomfortable feelings we listed first. For example, parents divorcing may make a teen feel rejected and abandoned. He or she may not be able to cope with new pressures at home.

The teen years are full of powerful and confusing emotions that can last a long time. Young people who say they want to die often think these painful feelings will never go away. They are

A few minutes after this picture was taken, this young man jumped to his death.

wrong. Working through these feelings may take a lot of time and effort. But it *is* possible to get help and turn your life around. For teens who are deeply troubled, there is no time to waste. For them it may be a matter of life or death.

Accident or Suicide?

Phil and Yolanda knew that something was wrong the minute they got off the school bus. Lights from ambulances and police cars were flashing everywhere, and emergency medical workers flooded the scene.

At the center of it all was the body of their friend Eric, lying facedown near the wreck of his motorcycle.

"Looks like he lost control," explained a police officer. "Probably just learned to ride."

But the students had a different story. "He was riding up the road to school," said Toni. "He looked at us and pointed as if he was saying, 'watch this.' Then he picked up speed and drove right into that tree."

"Oh, no!" Amber exclaimed. "Suicide?"

"He was pretty bummed about his grades," said Phil. "His dad was going to take away his bike if he didn't do better in school. And exams are this week. But who knows? Who'll ever know?"

The actual number of teenagers who commit suicide may be higher than the reported figures. This is because it can be difficult to determine whether a death was an accident or on purpose. If someone commits suicide without leaving a note, the death may be categorized as an accident.

People often wonder about the cause of some car accidents. A young person is alone in the car and crashes into something. The teen is killed. Upon inspection, the car had no mechanical problem and the teen was not under the influence of drugs or alcohol. Was it an accident? Maybe.

There are other suicides that we don't know about because people close to the victim often try to hide it. Many families of suicide victims will try to make the suicide look like an accident. They are ashamed that their child took his or her own life. They feel it says something bad about them.

But people need to know and face the truth about suicide. Maybe then it will be easier to stop suicide and suicide attempts.

Myths About Suicide

When you hear the word *myth* you might think of a story about imaginary people or events. The term myth is also used to refer to a mistaken belief or idea. This kind of myth can be dangerous because it may encourage people to take harmful actions. The following are a few of the common myths about teen suicide:

Young people who talk about killing themselves never really do.

Eight out of ten suicide victims told someone

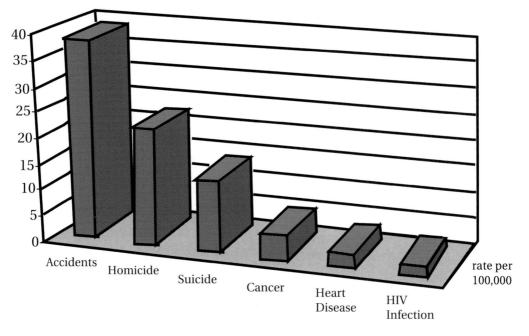

LEADING CAUSES OF DEATH
(15-24 YEARS OLD)

Source: U.S. Department of Health and Human Services, 1994 statistics

that they were planning to take their own lives. If someone you know says he or she is considering suicide, you should take it seriously. This person needs immediate help. You should encourage him or her to talk to a trusted adult. Or you could go to someone like a teacher, school counselor, minister, or rabbi for advice. They will be able to tell you how to help your friend.

Suicides usually happen without warning.

This myth is related to the first one. Most of the time, young people who are thinking about suicide *do* let someone know. If they don't say so directly, they might give out certain hints. For example, a teenager who is thinking about suicide might start giving away important personal belongings. He or she might start taking a number of unnecessary

20

risks. In chapter 3 we will talk more about some of the "warning signs" of suicide.

If someone really wants to commit suicide, no one can talk him or her out of it.

Remember, people who are thinking about suicide often do *not* truly want to die. They need someone to show them that they care and understand. They need to know they are not alone, even though they may feel like they are. Don't give up on teens who are considering suicide.

A person who seems to get better after trying to commit suicide will never try to kill himself or herself again.

Unfortunately, this is not the case. People who have tried suicide before are at risk of trying again. This does not mean that everyone who failed the first time will try again. But it does mean that anyone who has attempted suicide will need a lot of care and support afterwards.

Talking about suicide with an unhappy person can create dangerous ideas. Talking about it might cause him or her to try suicide.

If you think someone is considering suicide, you should always talk to him or her about it. You won't be putting ideas into his or her head. Remember, these young people *need* to talk about their unhappiness. People who are thinking about suicide often believe that no one knows or cares about how they feel. They need to be told that they are important. Your concern may give them strength to overcome their problems or find professional help.

Talking to a depressed person who is thinking about suicide can be tricky. Teens may be unsure what to say to help a friend. Comfort your friend and show you care, but before offering specific advice, it is always better to talk with an expert or a trusted adult.

Suicide is hereditary. If someone in your family commits suicide, you are likely to do the same thing.

If someone in your family commits suicide, this can certainly lead to feelings of depression and helplessness. But this does not mean you will want to take your own life, too. Suicide is not a trait passed down from one generation to the next. Suicide is always a choice. It happens when people decide to act on feelings of hopelessness and despair.

Finding Safe Solutions

If you feel that suicide is the only way to end your problems, try talking to someone. Find an older sibling, a friend, a teacher, a religious leader or any trusted adult. They can help you to see that

Police look for clues as to why four teens committed
suicide.

there are always other answers. If there isn't
someone around to talk to, or you prefer to talk
anonymously, call (800) 555-1212. Ask the operator
for a local suicide hot line number. Suicide hot
lines can also be found in your local telephone
book. Sometimes when you can talk about your
problem with another person, it may not seem as
bad as it did before.

Suicide is always tragic. The friends and family
of suicide victims will feel pain and grief for the
rest of their lives.

A powerful feeling of "aloneness" is common among teens who think about committing suicide.

Chapter 2

Losing Control

*L*uis was the skinniest eighth-grader in his class. He also wore glasses and had braces on his teeth, and the other students picked on him every day. They thought it was fun to push Luis into lockers and steal his money, because he was too weak to fight back. The teachers never did anything about it.

"I should just kill myself," he thought, "then they would be sorry." He pictured them all at his funeral, wishing they had been nicer to him. After one very hard day at school, Luis decided it was time to teach them a lesson. He swallowed about twenty sleeping pills. Then he just lay on his bed and felt glad that the other kids were going to regret making his life so hard.

Delita was a high school freshman who suffered from depression. Everybody feels low sometimes. Being sad is normal. But the depression Delita felt *was much worse than just a bad mood. She did not know why it happened, but about once a week she fell into a very deep state of unhappiness. It was as though all of a sudden, everything in her life seemed terrible. She would lock herself in her bedroom and sometimes cry for hours at a time.*

There were times when the pain Delita felt was so great that she wished she could just kill herself and put a stop to it. She told herself that if she could work up the nerve one day, she would commit suicide. She thought that death was the only thing that could end her suffering. Delita spent a lot of time feeling alone, wondering if anybody else ever felt so depressed.

Xavier replayed the moment over and over in his mind, watching the long, spiraling pass sail toward him in slow motion. It was his moment, the final seconds of the biggest football game of the year—if not the century. And he was wide open in the end zone. All he had to do was catch the ball.

Then suddenly he was grasping for the ball, watching it slip through his hands like a greased pig. Fumble!

Xavier cringed as the crowd's groan echoed in his head. How would he face everyone at school tomorrow?

Things would be even worse with Dad. All his father had ever dreamed of was watching Xavier play for the NFL. He had spent years working with Xavier, driving him to practices, paying for special coaching. How could he face his dad?

A rose and some photographs were all two young women left behind when they committed suicide. They left the motor running in a closed garage.

The pain felt by a suicide's family
never goes away.

*Maybe—he wouldn't. Dark thoughts flashed through
Xavier's mind. Game over . . . hopes over . . . maybe it
was time for his life to be over too.*

Frozen by Fear

These three young people are all in a great deal of
pain. One suffers rejection and humiliation every day
at school. Another has to cope with chronic depression, which may be caused by an imbalance of the
chemicals inside her brain. Still another lives in fear of
disapproval from his father.

Even though their problems are caused by different
things, the pain is equally strong for each person.
The strong feelings that Luis, Delita, and Xavier
experience make them feel as if they have no control
over their lives. The situation seems hopeless.

Think of what happens when a deer standing in
the road sees a car's headlights approaching. Instead
of running from the car, the deer stands frozen in fear.
The same thing can happen to people when they are
very afraid. They feel so overwhelmed by bad feelings
that they can't do anything to help themselves. They
can't think clearly and lose control over their emotions.
This sort of unclear thinking can lead to suicide.

If Luis were thinking clearly, he would realize that
killing himself is not a way to get revenge on his class-
mates. Even if they *do* regret being mean to him, Luis
won't be alive to see it happen. He is not thinking of
death as the end of his life.

Delita feels that her depression will last forever, but there is a good chance that it can be improved by therapy and medication. With help Delita may go on to live a happy, productive life. You must remember that death is a complete end—the end of things that are good as well as those that are bad.

Xavier thinks that suicide is an easy escape from his feelings of failure and stress. But he doesn't understand that life is a series of moments, some bad, some good. No one moment tells the whole story, and no one event defines a person's identity. Maybe Xavier and his father can come up with ways for his dad to show support without making Xavier feel pressured. If that doesn't help, there are always other people to talk to about these kinds of problems. Ending your life ends all opportunities to develop your strengths and show others what is special about you.

The Breaking Point

Sometimes an unhappy teen's problems can build up so much that they lead to a personal crisis. This moment is called the breaking point. A person may feel so overwhelmed that he or she stops thinking clearly.

The problem may begin at home. An alcoholic parent, for example, may be out of work and difficult to live with. Family problems may lead to other problems at school. With added stress the teen may turn to drugs or alcohol as an escape. As the problems get more

When a person is not able to keep problems from building up, it can become difficult to think clearly.

serious, he or she may be headed for a crisis. The teen could then begin to lose control over his or her emotions and turn to suicide.

Young people face pressures every day. Fortunately, most teens are able to handle crisis situations. Teens with good self-esteem believe in their own abilities to solve problems. They also know they can find help if they need it. They take control of their own lives.

Unfortunately, not all young people have such a healthy self-image. They may lack courage and confidence at a time of a crisis. They may feel helpless and unable to control the feelings that caused their crisis.

Feeling helpless in a crisis can make some

young people think about suicide. They begin to see suicide as a way out of their problems. Once they make the decision to commit suicide, they usually become calm. They no longer feel helpless, because they have decided to take action. Others may mistakenly think that these young people are getting better, and decide that they no longer need help. But this is the time when they will need help the most. If no one steps in to help, suicidal teenagers will try to end their lives.

The truth is, things *could* get better for troubled teens. But teenagers who think they want to die cannot see this on their own. When they reach a crisis, they need someone to reach out and show them a better way.

Suffering from Depression

Everybody goes through difficult times. While most people are eventually able to lift themselves from their sadness, there are others who have a much harder time. They find that they are easily trapped by their feelings. They may feel unable to see past their problems and realize that there is hope.

Many people who find that they cannot overcome their negative feelings may be suffering from an illness called depression. For them, depression may seem endless and uncontrollable. The reasons why some people suffer from

A person who has depression may feel tired or sluggish for long periods of time.

depression are not clear. It could be a combination of their experiences and the levels of certain chemicals in their brains.

There are millions of people who cope with this illness at some point in their lives. About one out of every twenty Americans suffers from depression. The symptoms can affect not only a person's emotions but also his or her physical health.

Because problems can feel much worse for a depressed person than for others, he or she will reach a crisis much more easily. People who suffer from depressive illnesses are the group most at risk for committing suicide. About 80 percent of suicidal individuals are severely depressed.

But depression does not have to lead to suicide. There are ways to treat depression, with both medication and therapy. If you think that you may be suffering from depression, a doctor or counselor can tell you how to get help.

Cluster Suicides

In recent years there have been a number of cluster suicides. In cluster suicides (also called copycat suicides) one or more troubled teens imitate another person who has committed suicide. They "copy" that person by killing themselves in a similar way.

Everyone is very sad when a young person takes his or her own life. But the sadness doesn't always end there. Soon afterward other students at the same school might take their lives in the same way.

Cluster suicides have happened in many towns across the country. The TV news reports a death in one state. Suddenly there are deaths like it thousands of miles away.

Copycat suicide doesn't even have to imitate an actual death. Even a story on television about teenage suicide can be followed by the real thing.

Looking for Attention

Some teens see suicide as a way to get attention. They see it as a way to be famous. But they don't understand that they won't be around to enjoy the attention or the fame. Maybe you have felt depressed enough to think about suicide. Or, the idea of trying to get attention that way may not make sense to you. Feelings of depression can keep a person from thinking clearly. It can make someone feel confused.

Troubled teens are more likely to get the help they need when the people who care for them can tell that a suicide may be coming. Fortunately you can learn how to spot the signs of suicide. The next two chapters will tell you how.

Chapter 3

Preventing Suicide

This book began with the story of Jordon and Kerry. If Jordon had been able to recognize the warning signs that Kerry was giving, he may have been able to get help for Kerry before she took her life. That does not mean that Kerry's suicide was his fault. But we can learn from their story about how to stop the people we love from ending their own lives.

Almost all people who consider suicide do not really want to die. They want to be helped and will send out signs to let others know. When these signs are recognized, action can be taken to prevent teenage suicide. The more young people learn about the warning signs, the better their chances of preventing a friend's or loved one's suicide.

Cries for Help

Sometimes, teens send very clear signals that they want to die. Here are some signs to watch for:

People who are considering suicide usually show warning signs.
One sign may be spending a lot of time alone.

Trying to commit suicide

The most obvious warning that a teen is suicidal is when the teen actually tries to take his or her life. Even if the attempt at suicide fails, it is an important sign. Just because someone has tried once and failed does not mean he or she won't try again. Anyone at this crisis point is at great risk. Getting professional help immediately is the only hope for making a lasting recovery.

Making threats or talking about suicide

If you know someone who is threatening to commit suicide, you should take him or her seriously. Most people who try to kill themselves tell someone, at some point, that they are thinking about it. Be a friend. Listen first, then get help.

Talking about death

Often, young people who are thinking about suicide will talk a lot about death. They may not talk about their *own* death—just the idea of dying. They may seem suddenly interested in methods of dying and the pain associated with each method.

Giving away favorite things

Teens who are thinking about killing themselves will sometimes give away their personal belongings. For example, a teen who loves music might give his friend his prized CD collection. Another young person might give away a favorite outfit or piece of jewelry or some other prized possession. In the story at the beginning of this book, Kerry gives her computer to her brother.

Taking unnecessary risks

Another way young people reveal that they are thinking about suicide is by taking unnecessary risks. Someone who never drinks alcohol or uses drugs might suddenly start abusing these substances. Or he or she might drink too much and then try to drive a car or ride a motorcycle. By taking dangerous risks, these teens are saying that they do not want to live.

Any behavior or conversations that are not normal could be a clue to a friend's true feelings. Pay attention to what you see and hear. It could save the life of someone you love.

Possible triggers: problems that add up

All teenagers go through rough times. Most get through these times without ever thinking about suicide.

But some young people may start to think about suicide when they reach a crisis point. If problems have piled up without relief, a teen may be headed for trouble. There is a limit to what a person can handle alone. When you or a friend feel overwhelmed, remember that help is always available. All you need to do is ask for it.

Some depressed teens are easily upset and may fight with their parents.

Depression: The Emotional Signal

It is normal to feel depressed, or very sad, from time to time. But most of us realize that it won't last forever.

Suicidal teens, on the other hand, are often seriously depressed for a long time. They *don't* understand that their depression won't last forever. In fact, most think it will never go away, and that death is the only way out.

Depressed teens often withdraw from their family and friends. They may seem very moody— happy and up one minute, sad and low the next. Or they may always seem bored and without energy. They might lose interest in the things they used to enjoy.

41

Depression, like suicide, has many of its own outward signs. The following are some warning signs of depression:

- No longer taking good care of himself or herself (wearing clothes that are not clean, not bathing or not keeping hair clean and combed; no longer caring what his or her room looks like).
- Not eating regularly, losing weight; or eating all the time, gaining weight rapidly.
- Drinking alcohol; abusing other drugs.
- Fighting with parents, siblings, even friends and teachers; not being able to control anger, or other strong feelings.
- Neglecting schoolwork, failing to attend classes.
- Spending less time with friends and family, and more time alone.
- Becoming undependable on a job; calling in sick day after day.

As we have seen, suicide does not happen suddenly. It is the result of negative feelings that build up over time. Identifying the warning signs can allow you to get help for someone before it is too late.

Chapter 4

Crisis Intervention

*T*he *phone is never allowed to ring more than twice here. Volunteer counselors answer on the first ring if possible. That's because they know that a few seconds can mean the difference between life and death.*

This is Lifepoint, a suicide hotline center in Minneapolis. From signs on buses that run past schools to radio ads read by rock DJs, Lifepoint uses the media whenever possible to broadcast its message to young people: "If you're thinking of ending it all, call us—anytime, day or night. We'll help you find a new beginning."

Counselors at Lifepoint, like all suicide hotline counselors, are trained to know what callers need to hear and to help them want to stay alive.

Suicide hotlines are telephone numbers that people can call to talk to a counselor about their feelings. It doesn't cost anything to call, and most hotlines can be reached at any time. Whenever a person is feeling alone or depressed, a crisis

Whenever a person needs to talk about his or her feelings, a counselor is always a phone call away.

counselor will be available to talk about whatever is troubling him or her.

Crisis centers are places where teens can go to speak with counselors about their problems. Counselors are trained to help them release all of the feelings they may be keeping inside. They use a method called crisis intervention or "CI." CI helps people deal with those strong feelings that can cloud clear thinking. CI has four steps that help people want to stay alive. Here are the steps:

Letting the feelings out.

Strong feelings are like steam in a kettle without a vent hole. The pressure builds up until the steam is ready to explode out of the kettle.

Crisis counselors understand these feelings. They know that feelings of anger, frustration, and loneliness shouldn't be bottled up inside you. Instead, they need to be released before you can think clearly about a problem. But first you need to know that it's all right to have these feelings before you can let them out.

Counselors let you know these feelings are normal. Everyone has them. Counselors are trained to understand these feelings. They want to show teens that someone knows what it's like to feel so angry and alone that you want to die.

Remember Kerry and Jordon from the beginning of the book? If Kerry had called a suicide hot line she might have told the counselor that her family had moved and she was having trouble making new friends.

The counselor might have answered, "That makes you feel very lonely and very angry at the same time, doesn't it, Kerry?"

Notice that the counselor did not talk about the move or Kerry's new school right away. She didn't try to cheer Kerry up. Instead she let Kerry know that she understood how she felt.

Being understood right away is often like a breath of air to a drowning person. Being able to release all of the emotions trapped inside can help you to view your problems more clearly. Then, you can begin to recover from feelings of anxiety or sadness.

Talking about the problem.

Once your feelings are out in the open, it is easier to talk about your problem. The counselor will then ask more about the situation. You may be a victim of child abuse or be pregnant. The counselor will not try to solve your problem. A problem may be too complicated to solve over the phone. Most problems are not easily solved at once. It usually takes some more time. The counselor is there to help you bring out all the facts. By recognizing these facts, you will have a clearer understanding of your problem. Then you can begin thinking about what part of the problem you want to work on solving first.

A suicide hot line counselor helps someone in crisis.

Taking one step at a time.

Trying to solve a big problem is usually much easier when you try to solve one small part of it at a time. In the same way, a counselor will help you look at all the parts of your problem. He or she will begin with the part that is easiest to solve.

A counselor might have helped Kerry by suggesting that Kerry talk with Jordon and the rest of her family about her feelings since their move. Kerry might have received some much needed love and support to help her get through the transition of moving to a new place. The counselor probably would also have discussed Kerry's difficulties at school.

Solving problems in several ways.

The final step in crisis intervention is to help the person see that most problems can be solved in several ways. In the case of fights with parents, for instance, a teen could ask an outside person to talk with both sides. The teen could move in with friends for a while. Another choice for the teen might be to do what the parents want but be allowed to ask something from them in return.

The important thing is for the teen to realize that there *are* other answers. When the teen knows that, he or she no longer feels trapped. He or she will probably no longer see death as the only way out.

With the help of the counselor and CI, you can begin to believe that there are other ways to solve problems. Counselors can help you to realize that you are not alone. There are people who can help you cope with the challenges of life.

CI is only one of the many options that can help troubled teens. Trained people are ready to help in schools, in youth clubs and neighborhood groups, in hospitals, and even in police emergency units.

Remember that CI and crisis counseling should be done by someone who is trained. Dealing with a suicidal person is a delicate matter because his or her feelings are so unstable. If someone you know is in danger of committing suicide, it is better to let a trained counselor handle the problem.

But there are some things a young person can do to help someone who shows signs of being suicidal. The next chapter tells what you can do to help.

Chapter 5

Reaching Out

*K*arla had promised to let her best friend, Jen, *in on a big secret, but now Jen couldn't believe what she was seeing. Hidden behind clothes, a corner of Karla's closet had been turned into a shrine, an "altar" for worshiping a rock star who had recently ended his life while in a drug haze. There were stories about his death cut from fanzines and tacked onto the wall. A shoebox was filled with poems that Karla had written about the star.*

"Mom and Dad never even let me play Rage's music," said Karla. "But from the way he smiled at me when I snuck into his concert, I know that we're soulmates. He wants me with him always."

From a drawer she pulled out a handgun that her dad kept for protection. "And after tonight I will be."

What would you do if your best friend said that he or she wanted to commit suicide? What *should* you do, or not do? Here are some guidelines to follow:

Friends often feel guilty for not noticing the early signs that can lead to teen suicide.

DO tell an adult—fast!

Whether it seems like a friend is or isn't serious about committing suicide does not matter. If they *say* they want to do it, there is a definite risk that they could actually kill themselves. There is really no "right thing" you can say that will stop your friend from committing suicide. It is best to leave the situation to an adult who is trained in preventing suicide.

You can find one of those adults by calling a suicide hot line. A hot line should be listed in the telephone book, or you can call information (555-1212) and ask the operator to find the number for you. School guidance counselors, doctors, or even the police can also be helpful. If you have friends and family that you trust, try talking to them as well. But it is best to find a person who is trained in handling suicidal feelings.

Do NOT try to handle the situation yourself

Trying to talk your friend out of suicide may make things worse because you may say the wrong thing. It is difficult to know what you should say to a person who is considering suicide. It is better to help him or her contact experts, like counselors or the police.

It is normal to want to help a friend. But trying to solve the problem yourself may do more harm than good.

DO remove all weapons or drugs

Some people mistakenly believe that by removing the methods of suicide, such as pills or razors, they are stopping the person from committing suicide. But, removing the means by which a person can commit suicide is only one step. The next step is to talk to an expert to find out how to help your friend.

Do NOT keep it a secret

Good friends are supposed to keep each other's secrets, but not if the secret is suicide! Tell an adult. Your friend might be upset at you for telling. But after he or she has been helped, your friend will thank you for it.

DO be a good friend

Be understanding and supportive, even if your friend is angry with you for telling an adult about his or her suicidal feelings. Try to stay in touch. Keep calling and visiting. People with problems need to know that others care.

When a person is feeling depressed, they might not be much fun to be around. But this is a time when your friend needs you the most. By knowing what to do, you can help your friend cope with his or her problems.

Chapter 6

Healing and Hope

Even with all of the resources available, suicides still occur. Every 110 minutes—approximately the amount of time it takes to watch a movie—someone between the ages of fifteen and twenty-four commits suicide.

For that person the problems are over. But for loved ones left behind, the problems are only beginning.

Anyone who has lost a loved one to suicide knows that this is one of the worst kinds of grief. It can be even more painful and difficult to handle than the loss of a friend to illness or an accident.

How do friends and families of the suicide victim feel after the suicide? How do they manage to go on? What do they have to go through before the pain and sadness can end?

Here are some of the feelings families and friends suffer when a young person takes his or her own life.

Friends and schoolmates have to try to understand the reasons for teen suicide. Then they can help prevent other needless deaths.

Shock

At first most family members and friends can't accept that a loved one killed himself or herself. They refuse to believe it. Maybe they knew about the victim's problems. Maybe they had heard threats of suicide. But they cannot accept that it has really happened.

The shock one feels after the loss of a loved one can be overwhelming. It is hard to think of other things and get on with one's life. This pain can make simple things like sleeping and eating difficult. This is a time when friends and family need help to heal and get their lives back to normal.

Sadness

Death always brings sadness, no matter how it occurs. For years a loved one has been there with you. You are used to the sound of a voice. You know the face. You know the touch of a hand. Now that person is gone forever.

No one can face that kind of loss without reacting to it. For a long time you might wish for the loved one to come back, even though you know that it can never happen.

People react in different ways to such feelings. Some cry. Others don't allow themselves to cry. Some want to talk about the loved one and the way he or she died. Others can't bear to talk about it. All people feel pain, though. Sometimes it seems like the pain will never end. It may seem to go away, but it returns suddenly upon seeing a picture or hearing a special song. With time, though, people learn to live with the loss.

Fear and Shame

Sometimes a suicide brings feelings of fear. Many people used to believe that suicide was a mental sickness handed down from parent to child. They feared that if one person in a family killed himself or herself, others in the family would do so too. Some even believed that the family was "cursed" and that suicide was bound to happen.

Now we know that this is not true. Just because you or another family member has attempted suicide, it does not mean that you are bound to commit suicide. A person who is depressed always has other options. These feelings can be resolved safely.

A suicide can also bring about feelings of shame. Family members and friends may feel ashamed that they did not know about the person's problems. Or if they did know about the problems, they may feel ashamed because they did not do enough to help the suicide victim. Family members may also be ashamed because they may believe that other people will see the suicide as a sign that something was wrong with the family.

Anger

Those left behind often feel great anger at the person who has committed suicide. "How could you do this to us?" they may ask. "Why did it happen?" "Why did you choose to die instead of coming to us for help?"

That anger often spills out into other parts of life. For instance, a child whose older brother or sister has committed suicide may suddenly begin to misbehave in school or have trouble with his or her schoolwork.

Guilt

Families and friends often blame themselves for the suicide of a loved one. They go over and over the last words and the last looks from the person. They try to think of anything they may have done to push the victim to suicide.

Coping After a Suicide

It is important for the families and friends of suicide victims to seek out professional help in their healing process. Counselors or other professionals can help by encouraging the family to talk about and explore their feelings. Families that do not seek help and bottle up their feelings may take a longer time to heal. Some may never heal at all. This can be dangerous because sometimes family members may become so depressed about the suicide that the family may begin to have other problems.

Counseling is also important in schools after the suicide of a student. Some schools have started suicide prevention programs. These may involve bringing in counselors to educate students and teachers about suicide, encouraging them to voice their feelings and talk to others about their problems. These counselors will also try to help students cope with the death of a suicide victim.

Schools may also set up peer counseling groups. These allow students to talk to each other about their feelings. Sometimes teens have an easier time expressing their feelings to others their age rather than to adults.

It is important that all people touched by a suicide have the chance to confront their emotions. Suicide can cause a crisis for anyone close to the victim. As we have discussed, these feelings might lead to other suicides. Counseling with psychologists or with peer groups can stop copycat suicides before they begin.

Don't wait for a death in your school, or your neighborhood. Remember the lessons you have already learned from this book. If you have problems or feelings that you can't cope with, get help from someone you trust. Tell him or her how you feel. And if a friend shares these kinds of problems or feelings with you, tell someone who can help you both.

While most teens never think seriously about killing themselves, the problem of suicide is very

School counselors can listen to students who need to talk about their problems.

real and serious. No matter what the number of teen suicides may be, the number of lives affected is much, much greater. As the problem of teen suicide is growing, many people are working to spread awareness about suicide. By learning what can be done to help yourself or someone you know who is depressed, you can help stop the growing number of suicides.

Glossary

child abuse Deliberate harm of a child by an adult.

cluster suicide Two or more teen suicides that happen around the same time or in the same way; also called "copycat suicide."

crisis When problems build up to a breaking point.

crisis center Place where trained counselors help people who are having problems.

crisis intervention Way to help solve an immediate problem.

depression Overcome by feelings of sadness.

emotion A strong feeling, such as anger, sadness, or happiness.

guilt Blaming yourself; belief that you are at fault.

heredity Passing on traits from parent to child.

hotline Telephone line answered by professionals trained to help with a problem.

myth A common belief that is not true.

shame Feeling as if you have done something wrong.

suicide The act of killing yourself.

victim A person who is in an accident, or a person who is the object of a crime.

weapon Gun, knife, or other instrument used to hurt another or yourself.

Where to Go for Help

For help anytime, day or night, use a **suicide hotline.** Call (800) 555-1212 and ask the operator for the toll-free number of a hotline in your area. You should be able to talk to a counselor over the phone right away. You can also look for a hotline mumber in your local telephone book.

Help is also available from the following organizations:

In the United States:
American Suicide Foundation
120 Wall Street, 22nd Floor
New York, NY 10005
(800) ASF-4042 (273-4042)
Web site:
   http://www.asfnet.org/

The Jason Foundation
116 Maple Row Boulevard,
   Suite C
Hendersonville, TN 37075
(888) 881-2323

National Institute of Mental
   Health (NIMH)
5600 Fishers Lane, Room 17-99
Rockville, MD 20857
(301) 443-3673
e-mail: nimhinfo@ nih.gov
Web site:
   http://www.nimh.nih.gov/

The Yellow Ribbon Program
Light for Life Foundation
   International
P.O. Box 644
Westminster, CO 80030-0644
(303) 429-3530
Web site:
   http://www.yellowribbon.org

Youth Suicide National Center
West Coast Office
1811 Trousdale Drive
Burlingame, CA 94010
(415) 573-3950

In Canada:
Canadian Mental Health
   Association
2610 Yonge Street
Toronto, Ontario M4S 2Z3
(416) 484-7750

For Further Reading

Axelrod, Toby. *Working Together Against Teen Suicide*. New York: Rosen Publishing Group, 1996.

Copeland Lewis, Cynthia. *Teen Suicide: Too Young to Die*. Hillside, NJ: Enslow Publishers, 1994.

Frankel, Bernard, Ph.D., and Rachel Kranz. *Straight Talk About Teenage Suicide*. New York: Facts on File, 1994.

Goodman, S. "Pulling a Friend Back . . ." *Current Health* 2 (February, 1991): pp. 18–19.

Kuklin, Susan. *After a Suicide: Young People Speak Up*. New York: G. P. Putnam's Sons, 1994.

Leenaars, Antoon N. (ed.), et al. *Suicide in Canada*. Toronto: University of Toronto Press, 1997.

Nelson, Richard E., Ph.D., and Judith C. Galos. *The Power to Prevent Suicide*. Minneapolis, MN: Free Spirit Publishing, 1994.

Slaby, Andrew E., and Lili F. Garfinkel. *No One Saw My Pain: Why Teens Kill Themselves*. New York: W. W. Norton & Co., 1996.

Smith, Judie. *Drugs and Suicide*. New York: Rosen Publishing Group, 1995.

Index

About the Author

Jay Schleifer has written more than forty nonfiction books for young readers, including several in the Everything You Need to Know series. Raised in New York City, he has been a public school teacher and was the editor of *Know Your World Extra*, a national classroom publication that received several EdPress Awards. Currently Mr. Schleifer is a publishing and editorial consultant and freelance writer working in New York and Chicago.

Photo Credits

Pp. 2, 24, 38, 44, 47 © Blackbirch Graphics; pp. 10, 32, 34, 41, 59 by Ira Fox; pp. 15, 17, 23, 27, 28–29, 50, 54 © AP/Wide World Photos.

Cover Photograph: Stuart Rabinowitz